Reflections of Faith
An Inspirational Verse Collection

Reflections of Faith
An Inspirational Verse Collection

Katie Sciabarrasi

Reflections of Faith

Copyright © 2014 by Katie Sciabarrasi
All rights reserved

This book or parts thereof may not be reproduced in any form, stored in a retrieval system or transmitted in any form by any means—electronic, mechanical, photocopy, recording, or otherwise without prior written permission of the publisher, except as provided by the United States of America copyright law.

Unless otherwise noted, all Scripture quotations are from the Holy Bible, King James Version.

Front Cover image copyright © by Rui Vale Sousa and used under license: Shutterstock.com. Cover image all rights reserved by the artist. Cover design by Katie Sciabarrasi.

First Printing 2014
Printed in the United States of America

Published by Spirit Life Media
Seagoville, TX 75159

www.reflections-of-faith.com

ISBN: 978-0-9906675-0-6 (paperback)

Spirit Life Media is a publisher of Christian inspirational works intended to uplift and exhort others to seek a deeper relationship with the Lord.

Ordering information: For details visit the website at www.reflections-of-faith.com.

U.S. trade bookstores and wholesalers, or others needing large quantity purchases: Please contact Spirit Life Media for discount information by email at info@reflections-of-faith.com.

This book is dedicated to my daughter Faelisa, who I love very much. To say that Faelisa had to face great hardship during her childhood is a vast understatement. Despite the challenges of her youth, she has grown into a beautiful lady with a compassionate heart. I want Faelisa and the world to know that I am proud of her and love her with all of my heart.

Acknowledgements

I would like to thank my dearest friend Diana Lugo for all her support and encouragement over the years. I greatly appreciate Diana's enthusiasm for the publication of this book and the books that are yet to come. Her thoughts and input as I prepared this book for publication have been priceless.

Most of all, I must acknowledge that without God's presence in my life and the guidance of the Holy Spirit, this book would not be possible. I often tell people that I am just the pen that God is using as the Holy Spirit breathes life into each poem that I write. To God be the glory.

Contents

PREFACE 9
  My Struggle to Find God 9
INTRODUCTION 11
  Reflections of Faith 11
THE EARLY POEMS 13
    He Took Your Place 14
    Jesus Is Love! 16
    What Manner of Love 17
    Finding Love 18
    What Is Christmas? 20
SPECIAL POEMS FOR SPECIAL PEOPLE 21
    A Gift From Above 21
    M O T H E R 22
    M O M (Words Can't Express) 22
    The Greatest! 22
    A Reflection of God's Great Love 23
THE LATER POEMS 24
    His Resurrection Power 25
    He Is Risen 26
    Let It Be You! 27
    Don't Let Me Take My Eyes Off You 28
    Another New Year 29
    Why So Much Sorrow, Lord? 30
    One Day At A Time 31
    Growing Pains 32
    Mixed Blessings 34
    Heart Song (Only Your Heart) 35
    Jesus, Mender of Broken Hearts 36
    His Hand 37
    Our Times Are In His Hand 38
    God Hears My Prayers 39
    Sit At My Feet 40
    Prove Me Now 41

- A House of Prayer 42
- Love Is 44
- Just Imagine 45
- What Really Counts 45
- Tried In the Fire 46
- It's Not Enough 47
- Feed My Sheep 48
- Worship In Truth 50
- A Decision for Life 52
- Only Truth 54
- Forgive and Forget 55
- Ugly or Beauty? 56
- Dressed In Christ's Glory 58

THE SPIRITUAL SONGS 60
- Jesus Loves Me 61
- Abiding In the Vine 62
- By Your Blood 63
- Peace 64
- Song of Thanksgiving 65
- I Will 66

WHAT DREAM IS IN YOUR HEART? 67
- Water the Seed With Faith 68

Preface

My Struggle to Find God

Here I am an ordinary person—just like everybody else. I have finally come to know God and I now know that He loves me, ordinary as I am. It had been a great struggle for me to give my life to the Lord. It's been a glorious victory for me since I have taken that step.

Life was full of disappointments and sorrow; a feeling of dissatisfaction, growing stronger every day. I had found the Lord as a young teen, but then I turned my back on Him and went my own way. Living life by choosing my will instead of God's will only caused a great deal of pain for my loved ones and me. So great was the pain and inner turmoil that I often thought of escaping the pain through ending my life.

When you live a life filled with sin and guilt, how can you feel joy in living? Yet the joy and peace were mine to have, but I couldn't find them alone. I finally realized that I needed to turn my life over to God's hands. Asking the Lord for His will to be done, instead of mine, lifted a great weight from my shoulders and brought the healing to my life that I so desperately needed.

I only had to ask and He filled my heart with His glorious peace...I felt His love for me touch the deepest part of my being. It was this love that I had been looking for in one relationship after another all those years when I was living in sin. Because He loved me first, I could finally love myself—something I was not able to do without Him. He forgave all my sins and washed my guilt and feelings of shame away...do you know what a blessing that is?

I can't praise the name of my Lord loud enough—even if I called His name from the highest mountain—it wouldn't be enough. Phrases and words fail to describe the goodness of my God! Now my life is so blessed, and though the everyday struggles of life go on—He carries my burden for me and fills me with His grace. I have faith that He will always be there for me, especially when I have a problem, and He never lets me down. When His answers to my problems are different than what I expect I remind myself that my heavenly Father knows what He's doing. I also remember how God has taken what Satan has meant against me for evil and brought blessings out of it.

I know that God has a great plan for my life and I believe He has given me a special gift with which to do His work. As I have studied the Bible, the Holy Spirit has revealed truth that has transformed my life. I began to write poetry that reflected the truths that the Lord had manifested to me, as enabled by the Holy Spirit. It humbles me and fills me with awe that God would give me such a precious gift and use it to touch the hearts and lives of others. It's my deepest heart's desire that others would come to know God and experience His love the same way that I have experienced His love! Lord God, please use each poem to bless the lives of precious people all over the world.

—Katie Sciabarrasi

Introduction

As this collection of poems began to grow, I soon realized that the words of comfort and encouragement that flowed from my pen were not meant for me alone. God birthed in me a strong desire to minister to the needs of others through each message He was giving to me. I pray you hear the voice of the Lord speaking to you, bringing refreshment, renewal, exhortation, and encouragement to you in whatever situation you may be facing.

The dream of seeing "Reflections of Faith" going forth as a published book has been hidden in my heart for many years. To see that dream become reality fills me with great joy as I anticipate how God might use the work of my hands to bring blessing into your life. I can think of no better way to introduce this work and to express what is in my heart than through the words of the poem which birthed the title for this collection.

Reflections of Faith

Reflections of faith...growing ever more dear,
The Truth that You give, the words that I hear...
Deep mysteries revealed by Your Spirit to me;
Your Word made alive are Your gifts to me!
The ears that can hear, the eyes that can see...
The Truth that You give that sets all men free...
Are precious and sweet; a great mystery...
And so undeserved are Your gifts to me!

No credit to me, it all is Your own...
For each of the lines, for each of the poems!
Every word of Your Truth Your Spirit reveals.
I'm only the vessel which Your Spirit fills!
To God be the Glory! You've written each one...
Every verse that I write; every song that I've sung!
So I humbly marvel at Your gift to me...
And I humbly thank You for love and mercy!

Reflections of faith...growing ever so dear;
Abounding...flowing over with each passing year.
Gifts that are given by Your Spirit to me,
Oh, how I praise and thank only Thee!
For the eyes that would see; for the ears that would hear:
Send forth Your Word and make it so clear!
Give them understanding and Your wisdom too.
Grant that they hear each message from You!

Let no heart be darkened; no heart be deceived...
For truth only enlightens when truth is received.
Send forth Your Word in the Spirit's power
To touch and to heal each one in this hour!
Let each heart know that they've heard from You
Because of Your mercy and love for them too!
For ears that can hear, and eyes that can see
The Truth that You give, will surely be free!

Reflections of faith...speak truth in my heart
To touch and to heal in my deepest part.
So the image of Jesus will become so clear
That others would see Him in me...and draw near!

(2 Corinthians 4:7) "But we have this treasure in earthen vessels, that the excellency of the power may be of God and not of us."

The Early Poems

The early poems focus on the love of God. Oh, if we could just wrap our head around the depth of God's love for us! When I finally experienced God's love for me personally, in the deepest part of my soul, my life was transformed. I never want to go back to the life I was living before God's love changed me!

We go through life looking for love. We all have a need for unconditional love. Many, (like me in the past) will look for love in all the wrong places and in relationships that end up bringing destruction to our lives. The Guardian of your soul is the only one who can truly love you unconditionally and *satisfy* your soul. He's waiting for you to reach out to Him.

God desires an intimate relationship with you and me. We *experience* His love when we shut out the clamor and commotion in our lives, and seek His presence. May you find love, joy, and peace in the presence of your God and Savior. The early poems focus on this love that I have experienced and I pray that as you read, you will hear God speaking, "I love you."

He Took Your Place

I have often thought within myself…
"How unworthy is my name,
That Jesus Christ should take my sin
And bear my guilt and shame."
How could Jesus look at me,
And see the value hidden deep inside,
That moved Him to such compassion…
That He suffered for me and died?
It was I who deserved to suffer…
It was my life that was full of sin:
And Jesus…whose life was sinless…
Opened His arms and drew me in.
With such love and compassion He said,
"Come unto Me…I will make you whole,
Take My yoke upon you…
And you shall find rest unto your soul."
My life was changed in that moment…
No longer in bondage to sin and shame:
Jesus set me free from the pig-pen!
And gave me a new life…a new name!
I know in my heart I have value,
Jesus values the whole human race.
He willingly died on a cross to prove it…
On a cross at Calvary He took my place.
An even greater wonder than this is
Christ's triumphant victory over death and sin!
My value grows daily through His power…
As my new life reflects Jesus within!
Have you ever questioned your value…
Are you low on your self-esteem?
Would Christ have died for something worthless?
Or is your value greater than it seems?
I know Christ suffered and died for you…
Have you believed the hardest part?

Perhaps you believe it in your head…
But have you believed it in your heart?
Have you seen yourself at Calvary's Hill
With drops of blood streaming down your face?
Did you realize deep in your heart…
It was for love of you that He took your place?

(Matthew 11:28-29 Jesus speaking) "Come unto me, all ye that labor and are heavy laden, and I will give you rest. Take my yoke upon you, and learn of Me; for I am meek and lowly in heart: and ye shall find rest unto your souls."

Jesus Is Love!

Trying to fill the emptiness?
No matter how you run from it,
No matter how you try…
You can't get away from it,
It's buried deep inside!
All the places that you look
For the love your heart is longing for,
And all those faces that you took
To be the one you needed…won't give you
What your soul is searching for!
Jesus is love! Jesus is love!
All the emptiness is gone now…
And my heart has finally found love…
'Cause I opened my heart to Him
And He poured all His love in!
Jesus is love!
My friend I know you're searching,
I can see it in your eyes—
Please believe me when I tell you
Only Jesus satisfies!
Please open up your heart to Him;
He'll fill that emptiness inside…
You won't have to keep searching,
Your heart will finally be satisfied!
Jesus is love! Jesus is love!
All the emptiness is gone now…
And my heart has finally found love…
'Cause I opened my heart to Him
And He poured all His love in!
Jesus is love!

(John 15:13 and 1 John 3:16)
"Greater love hath no man than this, that a man lay down his life for his friends…Hereby we perceive the love of God, because He laid down His life for us…"

What Manner of Love

It's because God loves you
That you're here today:
He's reaching out His hand to you
In a very special way.
It's because God loves you
And He wants you to know:
He uses our hands to hug, to touch—
His love to show.
God loves you and He's calling…
Calling out your name.
He knows all about you,
And He sees all your pain.
It's because God loves you,
That He wants to draw you near…
To become His son or daughter
And to cast out all your fear:
To fill you with His Spirit,
That you will be perfect in Him!
He wants to give you a new life,
No more bondage to sin!
It's because God loves you
That earnestly I pray…
For you to come to know Him…
To be Born Again today!
It's because God loves you
That He's come to live inside you!
But first let go of all yourself
So Jesus can wholly fill you!
It's because God loves you
That you're here today:
He's reaching out His hand to you
In a very special way.

(1 John 3:1) "Behold, what manner of love the Father hath bestowed upon us, that we should be called the children of God…"

Finding Love

Dear Heavenly Father, it is my prayer
Of praise and thanksgiving that I raise
For Your abundant mercy to me—
Dear Lord—to You be all the praise.
Your Holy Spirit guides me…
Keeps me safe from harm.
Your loving hands surround me:
Protect me from life's storm.
I can recount how many times
You've been a protective shield for me:
I see accidents—tragedies all around
In this great sea of humanity.
Every day I witness broken lives;
Sickness in bodies and in minds—
Souls searching for You unknowingly…
While endless blessings from You I find.
My body is blessed with good health—
I'm so thankful for this, You must see.
I've come so very close to harm—
But You would not let harm close to me.
You're always beside me,
Taking each step that I take.
You guide me with Your wisdom,
For each decision I make.
You are helping me to forget
The failures and sins of the past.
I'm inspired since my new birth in Christ—
I want this inspiration to last!
When I think of how I lived in sin
I ask—"How could You ever love me?"
But You loved me enough to buy my sin…
With Your own blood—to set me free.
I'm so in awe of Your great love—
Your mercy which knows no end.
You found my heart broken, then
My broken heart You did mend.

Why did it take me so long
To find my one, divine love?
When You were there all along—
Waiting for me up above.
I'm so glad that I did find Your love—
You waited for me so patiently.
Now I want to make up for lost time—
To love You, to serve You, for eternity.
If I could sing with a voice…
A voice that is strong and true:
Oh what praises I could sing—
For all honor and praise is for You.
I shall forever walk close to you
And this song of praise I'll raise…
To God be all the Glory,
And God be with me all my days!

(1 John 4:10) "Herein is love, not that we loved God, but that He loved us, and sent His Son to be the propitiation for our sins."

So often we hurry and scurry at Christmas time and the focus is only on the material aspect of Christmas—buying gifts, decorating, and going to parties. For some people Christmas time brings new feelings of isolation, loneliness, and depression. Others feel discomfort at forced reunions with family members for whom there are ill feelings. But God wants us to remember that Christmas is really all about His love for us.

What Is Christmas?

Christmas isn't mistletoe
Or tinsel on the tree…
Candy canes or cookies,
I hope that you'll agree.
Christmas isn't just bright lights
And gifts beneath the tree.
It's all these things…
But so much more…
Have you found the key?
Christmas is a precious gift
God gave to you and me.
Not wrapped in fancy paper,
But in a manger stall:
God sent His gift of love to us
That through His SON…
Forgiveness comes to all.
But if you've not received the gift
You've missed the dearest part…
For Christmas is not external…
It dwells within the heart!

(1 John 4:9) "In this was manifested the love of God toward us, because that God sent His only begotten Son into the world, that we might live through Him."

Special Poems for Special People

A Gift From Above

When you need a friend, someone to talk to,
When a heart reaches out to you in love…
That friend is a very dear treasure
Given to you as a gift from above.
For your need is seen not only by the eyes
And heart of the one He does send,
But also by the Great Provider, who in love
Touches you through your friend.
He speaks to our hearts and our minds,
About what a joy…it is to give.
He uses us to share the burden of others
To encourage them—to laugh, to cry, to live!
And everything we give to a friend,
He returns to us and even more:
"Pressed down and shaken together,"
His love flows from His never-ending store.
And the love He brings to a friendship,
We know will have no end…
'Cause when the Lord is the Lord of them,
Forever's not too long to live as friends.

(Proverbs 17:17) "A friend loveth at all times…"

MOTHER

M is for Mother, sweetest name to me…

O for one who gives herself…so self-lessly!

T is for your thoughtful ways,

H for helping hands,

E for your endurance…which through the years, still stands.

R is for recollections of you…so dear…

   growing fonder with each passing year!

(Proverbs 31:28) "Her children arise up, and call her blessed…"

M O M (Words Can't Express)

For all you've done
Throughout the years
T h a n k   Y o u!
Words can't express
How my life's been blessed
By your toil, sweat, and tears…
(And knees worn out in prayers),
But…T h a n k   Y o u!

The Greatest!

When it comes to Mommies
You're the Greatest!
Baker of chocolate chip cookies,
Player of peek-a-boo look-ies,
Tie-er of loose shoe laces,
Washer of bright, shiny faces!
Driver of car pool races,
In my book, Mommy you're aces!
When it comes to Mommies
You're the Greatest!

A Reflection of God's Great Love

A mother's love—a reflection of
A greater gift of God's Great Love;
As He gave she also gives—
Selflessly—she lives to see her son
Have joy and peace when all is done.
It is her will for him to know
The joy of Jesus who loves him so!
God gives her strength, to let him go.
It gives great joy and peace to know
Her son is in The Hands of ONE who loves him so!
Though it means a loss to her who holds him dear—
In her heart, she'll keep him near.
Her heart has heard God's spoken word—
Her mind too, has been reassured…
That God has chosen just the right ones…
The father and mother to bless her son.
In her heart and mind she knows—
He'll be just fine,
He'll bless their lives,
And be blessed with those
That God chose.
It gives great joy and peace to know
Her son is in The Hands of ONE who loves him so!
That depth nor height nor anything,
Can keep him from God's love and blessing!

(Rom 8:38-39) "For I am persuaded, that neither death, nor life, nor angels, nor principalities, nor powers, nor things present, nor things to come, nor height, nor depth, nor any other created thing, shall be able to separate us from the love of God, which is in Christ Jesus our Lord."

For all the unwed mothers who out of love for their child selflessly chose to give their child up for adoption to be loved and nurtured by another family. It is a heart wrenching decision that is fueled by self sacrifice. The sacrificial love demonstrated by these precious souls is truly a reflection of God's great love.

The Later Poems

This part of the collection focuses more on the Biblical truths as the Holy Spirit revealed them to me. Different themes can be found running through the poems in this section. The Holy Spirit has used these messages to bring encouragement when I have been discouraged, to remind me of what is really important, and yes, to even bring correction to my life when I have been outside of God's will. It is my prayer that God mightily uses this next section to transform lives as He has done for me. Dear Lord, I pray that You will cause Your truth to enter our hearts and use it to cause us to love You more and to bring greater liberty to our lives.

This section closes on the theme of forgiveness. One of the most important spiritual truths that the Lord has revealed to me has been the need to forgive others and to consistently walk in a state of forgiveness. As I began to apply this truth in my life (by the power and grace of God), I found that I was set free and deep wounds in my soul were healed. I was no longer a victim of those who had hurt me.

If I allow unforgiveness and bitterness to take root in my heart, then I open the door to the devil to take me into bondage *and to do every evil work (that he chooses to do).* We are warned in Hebrews 12:15, "Looking diligently lest any man fail of the grace of God; lest any root of bitterness springing up trouble you, and thereby many be defiled." Furthermore, we are warned in James 3:16, "For where envying and strife is, there is confusion and every *evil work.*" (Emphasis by the author).

I believe the Holy Spirit has caused me to minister about this truth because there are so many souls needing deliverance from the bondage of bitterness.

His Resurrection Power

The tomb is dark and silent,
The stone is rolled in place;
We mourn the passing of our Lord,
No more to see His face!
He said, "Father—forgive them,"
As He was by them crucified…
And He forgave His enemies
In those last moments before He died.
But we can't see beyond the facts…
He's dead—how can this be?
How can He save us now He's gone?
Where is the victory?
But wait—the tomb is open!
The stone is rolled away!
His shroud gives testimony to our hope;
Our Savior is risen today!
And in His Resurrection Power
Christ has won the victory!
He has fought the battle for us…
His power has set us free!
For as we die to ourselves
And surrender to His will…
We are given a new birth;
With His Holy Spirit—filled.
We experience the wonder of God's love
When in Christ we place our trust…
And through His Resurrection Power
We are alive in Christ and He in us!
And in His Resurrection Power…
Christ has won the victory!
He has fought the battle for us…
His power has set us free!

(1 Peter 1:3) "Blessed be the God and Father of our Lord Jesus Christ, which according to His abundant mercy hath begotten us again unto a lively hope by the resurrection of Jesus Christ from the dead."

He Is Risen

How awesome to think Jesus Christ, my Lord
Was sent by God according to His Word.
Because He loved me with a love so deep,
My soul from death He wanted to keep.
I can scarce believe He would send His SON
To free me from sin, after all I've done.
Not having a true relationship with God,
I walked in darkness upon this furrowed sod.
Jesus has led me out of the darkness into the Light.
I Love my Lord Jesus, in Him is my delight!
His gifts to me are love, joy, peace, and life eternal.
What gift can I give Him that is of equal value?
Nothing I possess could ever match His sacrifice…
The only gift I have—is to entrust Him with my life!
I asked Jesus to put me in the center of His will.
My life is His now—His wishes to fulfill.
Now I am His new creation, all fresh again—
The clay in the potter's hands; to be molded by Him.
Praise the Lord that He found me, when I was lost!
Praise the Lord for His victory over death on the cross!
The miracle of His victory over death was a promise
That I too could have, if I only have JESUS!
That's why my heart is so full of joy today…
It's the season of Easter—it's the Miracle of the day!
HE IS RISEN! What a glorious victory!
HE IS RISEN! From that cross on Calvary!

(Hebrews 2:9 and 4:14) "But we see Jesus, who was made a little lower than the angels for the suffering of death, crowned with glory and honor; that He by the grace of God should taste death for every man…Seeing then that we have a great high priest, that is passed into the heavens, Jesus the Son of God, let us hold fast our profession."

Let It Be You!

I need You oh, Jesus, I need you today.
Please let Your character come forth in me.
Everything that I do, everything that I say—
Let it be You that others see.
Let my "old man" be crucified
And deliver me from "self."
I try and try, but only fail—
I cannot change myself!
And how I long to be done with the old,
That I may be holy and perfect in Your sight…
I give You all my failures Lord,
For only You can make me "right."
My heart is yielded to Your will—
Oh, work Your perfect will in me…
And THANK YOU Jesus, that it's done—
Now I can see the victory!

(John 15:5b Jesus speaking) "…He that abideth in Me and I in him, the same bringeth forth much fruit: for without Me ye can do nothing."

Don't Let Me Take My Eyes Off You

Oh, Lord Jesus,
Don't let me take my eyes off You—
'Cause when I do,
Fears and worries overtake me…
Oh how they weigh me down!
You know when I look at circumstance—
(What appears to be…)
It multiplies the fears in me—
So, Lord Jesus,
Don't let me take my eyes off You!
Help me keep my eyes on You,
And lift this burden that I bear.
I need to let Your love surround me—
For Perfect Love casts out all fear.
Yes, Perfect Love casts out all fear.
I need Your love to reassure me—
You won't allow more than I can bear:
Help me to remember, Lord,
Those times You carried me when
I didn't know You were there!
Help me keep my eyes on You,
And lift this burden that I bear.
I need to let Your love surround me—
For Perfect Love casts out all fear.
Yes, Perfect Love casts out all fear.

(1 John 4:18) "There is no fear in love;
but perfect love casts out fear:
because fear hath torment."

Another New Year

He's just spoken to my heart:
"You have nothing to fear,
As you now face the unknown
Of yet another new year."

"For lo, I will be with you
Each step of the way,
So trust in My guidance:
Learn truth from Me today."

With such a different message
Than what the world believes…
Jesus teaches me the truth,
But how the world deceives!

I used to be caught up
In seeking what the world can give.
But now I'm seeking Jesus
And learning how to live.

For the things of the world
I have found in the past,
Have no eternal value…
There's no way that they can last!

But God's promises are true;
His truth will never fail.
With faith, I face the future
And God's truth will prevail.

(Psalm 119:160) "Thy word is true from the beginning: and every one of Thy righteous judgments endureth forever."

Why So Much Sorrow, Lord?

When tragedy comes into our lives and our hearts are shattered we don't understand why God allows such tragedy in our lives. It is the human condition to question God in times like these. Some will blame God, grow bitter towards Him, and turn away from Him. But wisdom urges us to cling to Him, to draw strength and comfort from Him. While I don't agree with the argument that Father God *causes* the tragedy, why He doesn't always shield us from it remains a mystery. (But I will minister in greater depth regarding this at another time). In my own life, I have both experienced great tragedy, and I have also been shielded from tragedy.

The greatest heartbreak that I have experienced was the death of my precious mother when I was only eleven. I felt abandoned by God because of her death and because of my lack of understanding. When I was sixteen, my life was shattered again when I was raped, and I blamed God, and turned away from Him. What I didn't know then that I know now was that evil powers were at work to attack me. The devil had two goals for me: to get me to turn away from God and to take me into bondage. He accomplished both of those goals through the attack on my soul. But after a period of twenty years, the Lord had mercy on me, called me back to Him, delivered me from the bondage, and brought healing to my life.

Why it took twenty years is a question that may never be answered. But knowing how great a miracle Father God did in my life gives me a deep sense of gratitude and a thankful heart for how God has worked in my life. I will *never* suggest that we should be thankful for the tragedy and sorrow that we must go through, but I believe that we can have a thankful heart towards the Lord for bringing us through the tragedy, and for the growth that we can experience because of it.

The next five poems in this section grapple with the question, "why so much sorrow, Lord?" I believe it is a question as old as time. In the poems, I hope that you will find words that encourage your heart if you are in the midst of tragedy, and that will help you see that you can have joy again. We are reassured of this as Psalms 30:5 tells us, "…weeping may endure for a night, but joy cometh in the morning."

One Day At A Time

At what yesterday might have been,
Don't look back with regrets and sorrow;
Look instead with faith and hope,
Towards a new and bright tomorrow.
No matter what you think, feel, or do:
You know you can't change past events.
So why do you keep on trying?
In truth, it makes no sense!
If you find the true Source of strength…
That enables our lives to change,
Your mistakes and failures of the past,
Become lessons…concisely arranged.
Spurring us on to new growth;
We draw strength from God's Spirit within:
As we listen to Him speak to us;
And we learn how to speak to Him.
Take it one step at a time —
It is a rough and rocky road.
Impossible, if God wasn't there by your side
To guide you and to carry the load.
The Lord's healing power will change you…
As you live life one day at a time.
The wounds of your heart He will mend;
And bring comfort and peace to your mind.
Don't try to live in the future —
Nor keep on grieving for the past.
He will bring about change in you slowly.
But the changes He brings surely last!
So live life expecting miracles!
Don't look for reason or rhyme.
So live this day as God shows you,
And take life one day at a time!

(Romans 8:28) "And we know that *all* things work together for good to them that love God, to them who are the called according to *His purpose*." (Emphasis by the author).

Growing Pains

We don't grow
When the going is good.
Although I know
We wish we could.
If every day is easy;
No struggle, no pain:
Over what do we triumph?
And what do we gain?
If we never see the darkness
How can we know the light?
And how can we appreciate
The stillness of the night?
Without a burden to be lifted,
We can't know "sweet release."
Without having turmoil—troubles—
We can't sense His Perfect Peace.
For when the going is good:
We tend to go our own way.
We seem to have less time for Him—
To have less time to pray.
But when the burden is heavy
And we turn to Him in prayer;
Our life in Him grows deeper:
'Cause we always find Him there.
As we draw into His presence,
He hears our every plea.
We come to abide in Perfect Peace,
When we seek Him continually.
Yes, it's in times of trouble,
Suffering, pain, and doubt,
That we develop deep gratitude:
It's the thing we can't do without.

A thankful heart is most needed,
So we can graciously receive…
All blessings great and small;
And appreciate our God and Lord,
The giver of them all!

(2 Corinthians 4:16-17) "For which cause we faint not; but though our outward man perish, yet the inward man is renewed day by day. For our light affliction, which is but for a moment, worketh for us a far more exceeding and eternal weight of glory."

Mixed Blessings

Life's disappointments and shattered dreams,
So many questions unanswered…
"Why are things never the way they seem?"
Just when you think you might have a chance
For that elusive state of happiness…
Fate comes along and throws it all askance.

Or is it God's way of letting us know
That we should be thankful for the good or bad:
The "mixed blessings" upon us He does bestow?
Because with the disappointment and the pain
We become humble once more and take our
Needs to Him, so peace we can regain.

And when it's "darkest before the dawn,"
We call upon our inner strength to get us through
The darkness, and to keep our will strong.
The light of hope will again shine for you and I
When we least expect it to…
We will again feel happiness; but will we ask why?

(Ecclesiastes 3:1 and 3:4) "To everything there is
a season, and a time to every purpose under the
heaven: A time to weep, and a time to laugh;
a time to mourn, and a time to dance."

Heart Song (Only Your Heart)

No other heart knows my heart's sorrow.
No other heart knows my heart's pain.
No other heart knows my heart's grieving.
No other heart knows my heart's shame.

Only Your heart sees my heart's affliction.
Only Your heart sees my heart's tears.
Only Your heart can bear my heart's sorrow.
Only Your heart can melt my heart's fears.

No other heart, but the heart of Jesus,
From its enemies, my heart defends.
No other heart, but the heart of Jesus,
Sends healing love, my heart to mend.

Only Your heart sees my heart hopeless.
Only Your heart knows how my heart weeps.
Only Your heart knows my heart is desperate
To receive the promise that Your heart keeps.

No other heart, but the heart of Jesus,
From its enemies, my heart defends.
No other heart, but the heart of Jesus,
Sends healing love, my heart to mend.

(Lamentations 3:41) "Let us lift up our heart with our hands unto God in the heavens."

Jesus, Mender of Broken Hearts

My heart was deeply touched
By a young man I've only met.
When I felt his broken, aching heart
I prayed for him and wept.
His head was surrounded by metal and bolts
Which pierced the flesh of his skull;
And the halo framed head and broken neck—
No movement of arms or legs at all.
Compassion urges me to reach out to him…
To say, "I know how you feel."
But though I may imagine—I know
I must experience for it to be real.
As I spoke with him briefly,
There were things I wanted to say…
That sometimes things happen to us
And we don't understand God's ways.
We don't understand why God gives us
Situations like this in our lives.
We're unaware of His great plan…
We don't see the world through His eyes.
"I want you to know that I understand—
My heart was once broken in two.
But Jesus' love mended my heart,
And that love can reach out to you."
Jesus is a mender of broken hearts;
He uses His great love to heal.
The love of Jesus deep within stirs
Me…to compassion—to love—to feel.
I carry a burden in my heart,
I didn't tell him what I had to say…
"Go ahead, be angry—cry out and grieve,
For God understands and it's okay."
After you grieve for your loss,
Comes a time for acceptance—thanksgiving;
For only God knows how His blessings keep flowing
To you…each day you are living.
(Psalms 30:5b) "…weeping may endure for
a night, but joy cometh in the morning."

His Hand

God works in mysterious ways
To unfold His plan…
He goes before us
To prepare the way,
He orders our steps day by day;
And though our hearts can't understand,
The puzzle pieces always fit
As they're put in place by His hand.
His hand will guide us
As we say, "Thy will be done."
He will cause us to choose
The right path—not the wrong one.
He'll gently lead us with His voice;
His Word will give us direction…
As we pray and listen…
And ponder in reflection.
He will bless our days with good,
No evil will come from His hand;
No mountain is too high to cross…
To keep us from The Promised land.
He has promised us a future,
And hope will overflow:
For God has a plan for us
That we will come to know.
Each day as we seek Him,
With our whole heart,
We'll come to know His plan.
He'll keep us always, (as we trust Him)
In the hollow of His hand.

(Jeremiah 29:11-14a) "For I know the thoughts that I think toward you (plans I have for you), saith the Lord, thoughts of peace, and not of evil, to give you an expected end (hope and a future). Then shall ye call upon Me, and ye shall go and pray unto Me, and I will hearken unto you. And ye shall seek Me, and find Me, when ye shall search for Me with all your heart. And I will be found of you, saith the Lord."

Our Times Are In His Hand

In His time…In His time…
He makes all things beautiful in His time…
We don't have to fret or worry
'Cause He's working day by day,
And He's surely come to show us
That He's made for us a way…
If we will only trust Him
And His will . . . seek to obey!
We don't need to fret or worry
'Cause His timing's never early:
Nor His timing won't be late
As we learn to sit and wait;
'Cause His timing's always perfect.
Just as nine months of gestation
Brings forth His new creation,
We will see the manifestation
Of His purpose and His plan!
Our times are in His hand,
So let us live one day at a time:
Lean not on our own wisdom,
But seeking first His kingdom;
And all other things we need…God will supply.
He fed Elijah one day at a time…
The ravens fulfilled His plan.
Will He not do the same for us,
If He can do such a thing for this man!
For Elijah was just like us:
Just an "ordinary" man…
But You called him to Your purpose,
And You chose him for Your plan.
And if we…like him…
Should find favor in Your sight:
We pray, reveal to us Your Glory;
And reveal to us Your might…
For our times are in Your hand
Both day and night!
(Psalm 31:15a and 37:5) "My times are in Thy hand…Commit thy way unto the Lord; trust also in Him; and He shall bring it to pass."

God Hears My Prayers

When life seems to be a struggle,
When there's no place else for me to go—
You are a sanctuary in the storm,
A trusted friend who I love so.
I'm so thankful that God hears my prayers.
Everytime I ask the Lord for something
In Jesus' name, He is always there.
If the world should turn its back on me,
I still have nothing to fear:
Because You will always be the rock
On which I can shed my tears.
I'm so thankful that God hears my prayers.
Everytime I ask the Lord for something
In Jesus' name, He is always there.
I love to walk the paths that Jesus led,
But sometimes I stumble and fall…
Then You pick me up to walk straight again,
And I rejoice to hear my Master's call.
I'm so thankful that God hears my prayers.
Everytime I ask the Lord for something
In Jesus' name, He is always there.
With boundless mercy, You forgive my sins.
My life is so blessed in many ways…
I have put my faith in You, Dear Lord:
To keep me safe through all my days.
I'm so thankful that God hears my prayers.
Everytime I ask the Lord for something
In Jesus' name, He is always there.

(1 John 5:14-15) "And this is the confidence that we have in Him, that, if we ask anything according to His will, He heareth us:
And if we know that He hear us, whatsoever we ask, we know that we have the petitions that we desired of Him."

Sit At My Feet

You're pulled in many directions
Encumbered and weighed down…
Your cares have become a whirlpool,
And you are about to drown!

First, "This" calls for attention…
And "That" screams your name;
But I call you oh, so quietly…
My voice is not the same.

I say, only one thing is needed.
Come, and sit apart…
Sit, and listen at My feet—
Let me speak to your heart!

Unless you come, sit at my feet,
You will not hear My voice;
You have to choose what's needed…
You have to make a choice.

(Luke 10:39 and 41-42) "And she had a sister called Mary, which also sat at Jesus' feet, and heard His word. And Jesus answered (*Martha*) and said unto her, Martha, Martha, thou art careful and troubled about many things: But one thing is needful: and Mary hath chosen that good part, which shall not be taken away from her."

Prove Me Now

Prove Me now in this:
Not just a month or two or three…
But all throughout your life,
You'll see how faithful I can be!
Bring your tithes into the storehouse,
Clearly hear My word in this:
Purpose in your heart to hear Me,
And My Will you will not miss.
Have I not said, "I'll feed you,
And meet your every need?"
I call you now to trust Me:
Because others I would feed…
My harvest fields stand waiting;
My Spirit searches out the needs:
Your tithes and gifts are an offering
Of faith: They are planted seeds!
Will I not bring forth a harvest
In which you can rejoice?
Will I not pour out My blessings;
If you will only hear My voice?
It is a step of faith in Me:
A step of obedience too.
Have I not said, "You can test Me in this:
To bring forth what I've promised to you?"
I Am a rewarder of those who seek Me,
And purpose to obey My will.
I Am your All Sufficiency.
There's no need I can't fulfill.
My Spirit calls you to remember…
You said—you gave your life to Me.
My Spirit calls you to remember…
Nothing—would I withhold from thee!

(Malachi 3:10-11a) "Bring ye all the tithes into the storehouse, that there may be meat in mine house, and prove Me now herewith, saith the Lord of hosts, if I will not open you the windows of heaven, and pour you out a blessing, that there shall not be room enough to receive it. And I will rebuke the devourer for your sakes…saith the Lord of hosts."

A House of Prayer

In the still and quiet of darkness
I bow my head and pray.
I listen to hear Your voice
At the start of each new day.
Your house shall be called
A house of prayer…
When Your people remember
We can call on You there!
The temple in which You live
Is not made with mortar and stone.
For this living temple—my body…
Was created for God alone.
Your house shall be called
A house of prayer…
When Your people take time
To meet with You there!
With each supplication and plea,
Comes the assurance that You hear:
As I lift my voice to heaven,
And lift my heart in prayer.
Somehow, You amaze me still,
As You remind me in Your Word;
That as I diligently seek You,
My prayers are always heard.
Sometimes my heart is burdened
With those who don't know the way:
Then I hear Your Spirit prompt me,
"Just bow your head and pray."
Sometimes I cry out for mercy,
Convicted of my sin…
And Your grace and Your forgiveness,
Like opened arms…draw me in.
Sometimes too, my fears overcome
As I face the unknown of today.

Again, I hear Your Spirit,
As You gently say, "Just pray!"
Other times, I face problems…
I'm sure there's just no way!
But You supply what is needed,
If I just bow my head and pray.
And times I know not often enough,
I kneel and bow to say:
Thank You for all You've given,
And for teaching me to pray!
When I need guidance…direction,
For each and every new day;
There is no other source but You…
All I have to do is just pray!
When I take the time to draw near,
I find joy in being with You!
For You delight in this temple…
A house of prayer and worship too.
Your house shall be called
A house of prayer…
When Your people draw near
To worship You there!

(Romans 12:1 and Isaiah 56:7b)
"I beseech you therefore, brethren,
by the mercies of God, that ye present
your bodies a living sacrifice, holy,
acceptable unto God which is your
reasonable service."
(The Lord speaking) "…for mine
house shall be called an house of
prayer for all people."

Love Is

It's not true that love is
Never having to say you're sorry:

For we are human and make mistakes.
Love is—saying and meaning "I'm sorry."

When it is true love you will find,
Love is patient and love is kind.

Love is all those wonderful things
You would like others to do for you…

That you give to someone else…
As a gift of yourself—it's true.

Love is gentle, giving and sweet;
And giving your love to others
Will make your life complete.

To be unto others as was Jesus Christ,
And to mold your life after His:
Is the true measure of what love is.

 (I Corinthians 13:4-6)
"Charity suffereth long, and is kind;
charity envieth not; charity vaunteth
not itself, is not puffed up, doth not
behave itself unseemly, seeketh not her
own, is not easily provoked, thinketh
no evil; rejoiceth not in iniquity, but
rejoiceth in the truth…"

Just Imagine

Wouldn't I grow dissatisfied and jaded
If God granted my every whim and wish?
Just imagine how boring life would be
If my appetite was always sated.

I would not experience the great pleasure
Of dreaming dreams and pursuing them;
Or of meeting the challenges of life;
For it is in the challenge where lies the treasure.

I hope to never lose the sense of joy inside
And feelings of satisfaction from a job well done.
I can contribute something of value to this earth
With God's loving guidance ever at my side!

I must dare to dream and pursue my dreams…
"To reach out and touch a human life," is one.
Just imagine how fulfilling life would be
To have realized a goal with such a theme.

(Philippians 2:13) "For it is God which worketh
in you both to will and to do of His good pleasure."

What Really Counts

My years are almost full…
A little time left to do.
Grant me Lord, a soul
Or better yet…a hundred, two!
For nothing in this world
Counts for eternity…
But seeking to save the lost…
And finding more love for Thee!

Tried In the Fire

You're dealing with my heart, Lord,
Those secret sins that no one sees.
Like spiritual pride, my judgment of others;
And failing to love them unconditionally.
You're cleaning out the closets
As I open each door to let You in.
The gentle knock of Your Holy Spirit
Beckons me to see my secret sin.
I know I'm being tried in the fire, Lord;
That You would remove all impurity—
And cause only pure gold to remain
So that "only You" is seen in me.
It's not easy being tried in the fire,
It's not what my flesh would choose—
But my spirit desires to be as Jesus,
So try my flesh, that it be removed.
Being tried in the fire is what I desire
Because I hold nothing back from You.
My flesh so often gets in the way
Of loving others the way You do.
You've called me to a holy calling
That only You can fulfill—
To love my neighbor as myself,
But the flesh is weak, though the spirit wills.
And my flesh wars against my spirit
So how do I perform Your will?
I cannot do it! Lord, You've shown me—
Only Your life in me, as the branch in the tree
Can bring forth the fruit of Your will!
And I know You are faithful to keep
That which I have entrusted to You—
So I give You the desires of my heart, Lord—
That I <u>can</u> love others as You do!

(John 13:35 Jesus speaking) "By this shall all men know that ye are my disciples, if ye have love one to another."

It's Not Enough

Oh Lord, You know
My heart overflows
With gratitude to You.
Your "Amazing Grace,
How sweet the sound,
That saved a wretch like me!"
But Lord You know
It's not enough,
That my soul is born anew…
For so many that are lost…
All around me I see;
Stumbling in the darkness
From which You delivered me;
Searching for true love…
Living lives of futility;
Giving their souls away to Hell
With eyes that cannot see.
It's not enough that my heart knows
That Love is found in You…
There are so many others
That need to find love too.
To share the words You give,
I need my heart to be more bold!
I need a heart to pray and pray…
To free them from sin's hold.
It's not enough to know
That I'm the object of Your Grace…
For I want them to be with me
When I get to see Your face!
It's not enough to know
That I'm the object of Your Grace…
For I want them to be with me
When I get to see Your face!

(Matt 18:14 and Luke 19:10) "Even so it is not the will of your Father which is in heaven, that one of these little ones should perish…For the Son of man is come to seek and to save that which was lost."

Feed My Sheep

Father, forgive them…for
They know not what they do.
Father, forgive them, and help me…
I want to forgive them too.
They don't know that this little girl
Is a test for us, sent by You.
They have rejected her, judged her…
But, they say that they have loved her.
They responded to this child "in trouble"
With fear she would be a wrong influence:
"We're sorry she feels rejected, but…
It's just part of her consequence."
I believe they have forgotten Lord,
That ours is not to judge.
I believe they have forgotten that
Jesus taught us how to love.
This is the Lord's commandment,
(His unconditional love is true)
"That ye love one another
Even as I…have loved you."
I believe their spiritual vision
Has somehow grown very dim.
They have responded to her in the flesh;
Not by the power of the Spirit within.
Open their spiritual eyes, Lord
So that they might see…
That by Your Perfect Will
You've allowed all this to be.
Don't let them be deceived, Lord—
Let them have faith, not doubt.
Holy Spirit help them love her
That Your blessings would pour out.

Jesus said, "Simon, do you love Me
More than these—then feed My sheep."
"Simon, do you truly love Me
More than these? Feed My sheep."
She is one of the Lord's lost lambs
Won't you feed her now?
Just ask our Father for wisdom…
I know He'll show you how.

(1 John 3:17-18) "But whoso hath this world's good, and seeth his brother have need, and shuteth up his bowels of compassion from him, how dwelleth the love of God in him?…Let us not love in word, neither in tongue; but in deed and in truth."

Worship In Truth

Search my heart—Holy Spirit;
Reveal any darkness to me.
Cause Your light to shine on my heart…
And cause any darkness to flee!
Search out the deep recesses:
Any sin that I can't see.
Expose sin by the light of Your Word…
By Your Word reveal truth to me!
Sanctify me by Thy Truth;
For Thy Word is truth indeed.
Quicken the truth by Your Spirit…
For on Thy Word I must feed.
If I would spend time in Your Presence:
A pure heart is what I need…
That I may know You and praise You;
Worship You in truth and in deed!
For the Father seeks such as these:
To worship Him in spirit and truth.
For the days of this age grow short,
And grace will soon turn to wrath!
But while it is still today,
Let me not harden my heart:
I'm washed with the Precious Blood,
Let it touch me in my deepest part.
Oh, let my heart never forget
What Your gift to me cost You!
Let my heart always desire
To be made in Your likeness too!
For as I become like Jesus,
From glory to glory I will see
Truth manifested in my life…
As His image becomes clear in me.

I then will worship my Father
And sing praises at His throne.
With my whole heart I will worship…
Only God…And God alone!

(John 4:23-24; John 17:17 Jesus speaking) "But the hour cometh, and now is, when the true worshippers shall worship the Father in spirit and in truth: for the Father seeketh such to worship Him. God is a Spirit: and they that worship Him must worship Him in spirit and in truth." (Jesus praying for His disciples) "Sanctify them through thy truth: thy word is truth."

A Decision for Life

Life is so short and you don't even know it.
You fit in mother's lap; but then you outgrow it.
No longer a child, not yet of the adult class...
With sensitive feelings, and a heart of glass
You face decisions: What to study; what to wear
And even how to style your hair.
You want very much to fit in, this is true,
And yet, to remain, uniquely you.
There are so many choices all around...
Do you sometimes feel you are losing ground?
Do you ever feel you just want to give in,
Beause you feel no hope that you can win?
You are faced with inner struggles every day,
As situations in life come into play.
"It's time you grew to know, who you really are!"
"Where are you going," you ask, and "will you go far?"
"What do you want to do with your life?" you ask,
"Can you show your true self, or must you wear a mask?"
You gain friends, you lose friends, you move away...
Conflicts arise because you have no say.
You're sure your parents don't understand...
The conflicts may grow; may get out of hand.
You talk to your friends; they have no solution.
They may be in the same boat, in the same ocean.
Is there no help, no way out of your despair?
Can you find reassurance; someone to care?
If you seek security and someone to love you,
Be assured and know He is waiting above you.
Is there someone to really love you—out there?
How can you find Him in that great somewhere?
He is waiting for you—to call out to Him;
To say, "I love you, Jesus, won't you please come in;
Come into my heart; please show me the way,
To find the peace of mind I need so much today.
Please Jesus, heal my lonely, aching heart,
Lift my burdens, and from me, don't depart."

Be assured, as soon as He hears your call,
Your loving shepherd Jesus, will not let you fall.
He is a dear friend, whom you can always talk to,
But—listen closely, to what He will tell you.
He will show you how to fill your life with joy.
No matter who you are, no matter girl or boy.
He will help you find and know your true self.
In this troubled world, He'll fill your life with wealth.
He'll fill your heart with peace—take your pain away.
Don't wait, ask Him now; call out to Him today.
He's waiting to hear from you—He's there—
Wanting you to lift your heart to Him in prayer.

(Jeremiah 33:3) "Call unto Me, and I will answer thee, and show thee great and mighty things, which thou knowest not."

Only Truth

Angry words fly…
But crying deep inside.
Feelings of rejection…
Surface—will not hide.

Spirit of Bitterness
Rises up again.
And Unforgiveness…
His companion,
Take hold of me and then:
Once more resentment
Boils hot and fast!
But yet, within my spirit…
Longing…for Truth at last!

Only Truth can break this bond;
Only Truth can set me free
From this hold…so strong.
Release of forgiveness
Face to face…
Remembering who I am…
Object of Your mercy…grace!

Forgiving, as I am forgiven too,
That is Truth—revealed to me.
Enabling power comes from You!

(John 8:31-32 and Colossians 3:13)
"…If ye abide in My word, then are ye
 My disciples indeed; and ye shall
know the truth, and the truth shall
make you free…Forbearing one another,
and forgiving one another, if any man
have a complaint against any; even
as Christ forgave you, so also do ye."

Forgive and Forget

If looking back in time only causes us pain,
And keeps our wounds from healing—why do we
Keep those memories alive again and again?

Can't we put them on a shelf, there to remain?
To give our hearts a chance to forgive—
Instead of stirring them up, to renew our hurt again,

Why can't we let the Lord into our minds and hearts
To let His healing powers touch our lives?
Unless we forgive, it will surely tear us apart.

I'm truly sorry for the wrong things I have done:
Whether it be through thought, word, or deed.
I'm sorry for the strife—neither one of us has won.

I do feel in my heart, all the pain that is yours…
And my own pain as well, you can believe—so let's
Choose to forgive…put strife behind closed doors.

Let the Lord's healing power come into our hearts,
So we can then choose to forgive and forget…
And God's helping hand will accomplish His part.

(James 3:14 and 16) "But if ye have bitter envying and strife in your hearts, glory not, and lie not against the truth…For where envying and strife is, there is confusion and every evil work."

Ugly or Beauty?

Bitterness is ugly…it goes
Much more than skin deep:
In the very depths of your soul,
A festering wound it would keep.
Forgiveness has a great beauty
And healing powers too…
That reaches into the heart of a man
And brings forth forgiveness for you.
For has the Lord not told us,
To freely give the same gift?
When our sins nailed Him to the cross
And His blood crossed over the rift?
His blood purchased our forgiveness:
And the chasm between God and man—
Was bridged by His atonement and left us
To be found in His Presence—to stand!
Because of the gift of forgiveness—
We can seek Him face to face…
Because we sense that His forgiveness
Is matched only by His Grace!
And has the Lord not told us
That we must freely recognize;
That if we don't give forgiveness…
Our own forgiveness we despise?
Would you regard it as not precious;
A cheap and frivolous thing?
Or would you regard it as holy…
From the Lord's hand a great blessing?
Give and it shall be given…
Pressed down and overflowing too—
For with the same measure you give it,
Forgiveness comes back to bless you!

Bitterness is so very ugly…
And a cancer to the soul…
It defiles and destroys all it touches;
None who own it can be whole.
If we will be set free from it:
We first must recognize—
That if we don't give forgiveness,
Our own forgiveness we despise!

(Psalms 32:1 and Ephesians 4:31-32)
"Blessed is he whose transgression is forgiven, whose sin is covered…Let all bitterness, and wrath, and anger, and clamor, and evil speaking, be put away from you, with all malice: And be ye kind one to another, tenderhearted, forgiving one another, even as God for Christ's sake hath forgiven you."

Dressed In Christ's Glory

You say you are a Christian?
One who follows how He lived?
Then I ask just one more question:
Why do you not forgive?
You say you are named after Christ,
That you are a follower of His?
That you follow His example;
What He teaches and how He lives?
If the Holy Spirit abides
Within the body of Christ today;
Where is the power that He gives
To enable the church to obey?
If the Holy Spirit has come
To bring love and unity…
To make all parts of the body one,
Why do we grieve Him continually?
He said, "By this will the world
Know that you belong to Me:
If you have love one for another…
And live in truth and harmony."
He said, "By this will all men see
The glory of God in you:
When you lay down your lives for each other,
And lay down your bitterness too."
It is the one sin that remains
So strongly ingrained in you,
To break down your relationships;
To keep you from being renewed.
He said, "Husbands, love your wives,"
This is the Lord's word to you.
But how many husbands fail to see,
That love can't live with bitterness too.
And how many wives fail to forgive
When the husband fails to obey?
There has to be another answer…
There has to be a better way!
Unforgiveness is the one sin
Our Father said He will not forgive.

It is a very strong word to us,
We must embrace if we're to live:
In truth and harmony
And in the Spirit's power;
In love and unity
Now in this final hour!
For the days are growing short,
And Christ is coming soon…
To come and call His own
To finally take them home.
Will you be left standing there,
In that final hour?
Because you have not yielded
To the Spirit's word and power?
Or will you be bathed in glory
As you see Him face to face?
As He calls you as His very own,
Because you yielded to His grace!
Forgiving, as we are forgiven too:
Is the truth we need to live.
The choice is ours to make…
The power to obey is the gift He gives.
If you would see bitterness as the sin
That might keep you from Christ's side;
Would you not search your heart today,
To be washed in the cleansing tide?
The Spirit searches out our hearts…
We have only to invite Him…
To show us where our bitterness lies
And give us power to forgive them.
So when the final hour has come,
We'll be truly dressed in Christ's glory!
Because His glory has been revealed
Here on earth in our own life's story!

(John 12:48; 2 Chronicles 7:14) (The Lord speaking) "He that rejecteth Me, and receiveth not My words, hath one that judgeth him: the word that I have spoken, the same shall judge him in the last day…If My people, which are called by My name, shall humble themselves, and pray, and seek My face, and turn from their wicked ways; then will I hear from heaven and will forgive their sin, and will heal their land."

The Spiritual Songs

This section is the collection of the songs that the Lord has given to me over several years. Some of the melodies came to me at the same time as the words, while other melodies came to me weeks or even months later. While you won't know the melodies, I pray that these song lyrics will minister to you as powerfully as they have to me. This section actually starts with "Jesus Loves Me," which is a song with which most of us are familiar. But one day the Lord gave me new lyrics to go with the ageless melody of "Jesus Loves Me." Sing it to yourself often!

Jesus Loves Me

Jesus loves me, this I know,
For He has already shown me so!
This little one to Him belongs,
I am so weak, but He is strong.
Yes, Jesus loves me!
His love has no end.
Yes, Jesus loves me!
On Him I can depend!
Jesus loves me—have you heard?
He's spoken to me this very word!
By His blood…He shed for me,
Jesus has shown His love for me!
Yes, Jesus loves me!
His love has no end.
Yes, Jesus loves me!
On Him I can depend!
Jesus loves me even when I fall,
And His love speaks…when I call…
For His blood that was shed for me
To cover my sin and set me free!
Yes, Jesus loves me!
His love has no end.
Yes, Jesus loves me!
On Him I can depend!
Jesus loves me…He's come to heal…
Every heart ache that I feel…
Every fear my heart believes,
His loving presence now relieves!
Yes, Jesus loves me!
His love has no end.
Yes, Jesus loves me!
On Him I can depend!

(John 15:9 Jesus speaking) "As the
Father hath loved Me, so have I
loved you: continue ye in My love."

Abiding In the Vine

I chose you first; you chose not Me…
I chose you and made you My own.
I chose you first; you chose not Me…
I chose you and made you My own.
Stay close to Me…stay close to Me…
You cannot bear your fruit alone!
Stay close to Me…stay close to Me…
You cannot bear your fruit alone!
Abiding…abiding…
Abiding in the vine!
Abiding…abiding…
Abiding in the vine!
Be crucified…be crucified…
Be crucified that you might live.
Be crucified…be crucified…
Be crucified that you might live.
Unless you die…unless you die…
I cannot live My life through you;
Unless you die…unless you die…
I cannot live My life through you!
Abiding…abiding…
Abiding in the vine!
Abiding…abiding…
Abiding in the vine!
Abide in ME—and in My Word…
Apart from ME you have no power!
Abide in ME—and in My Word…
Apart from ME you have no power!
Abiding…abiding…
Abiding in the vine!
Abiding…abiding…
Abiding in the vine!

(John 15:4 Jesus speaking) "Abide in Me, and I in you. As the branch cannot bear fruit of itself, except it abide in the vine; no more can ye, except ye abide in Me."

By Your Blood

You are Holy...You are Holy...
And by Your blood I am holy too.
You have bought me...You have changed me...
And by Your blood I am made brand new!
I claim Your blood to cover me...
To shield me from my enemies...
To give me power to overcome!
And rise triumphant when all is done!
You are Jesus...The God who heals me...
And by Your blood all my wounds are healed.
You are Jesus...The God who chose me...
And by Your blood my life in You is sealed!
I claim Your blood to cover me...
To shield me from my enemies...
To give me power to overcome!
And rise triumphant when all is done!
You are Jesus...The God who knows me...
And by Your blood I can know You too.
You are Jesus...The God who sees me...
And by Your blood I'm beginning to see You!
I claim Your blood to cover me...
To shield me from my enemies...
To give me power to overcome!
And rise triumphant when all is done!
You are Jesus...You brought truth to me...
And by Your blood this captive is set free!
You have overcome...Every enemy!
And by Your blood I have the victory!
I claim Your blood to cover me...
To shield me from my enemies...
To give me power to overcome!
And rise triumphant when all is done!

(Revelation 12:10-11) "And I heard a loud voice saying in heaven, Now is come salvation, and strength...for the accuser...is cast down...And they overcame him by the blood of the Lamb, and by the word of their testimony; and they loved not their lives unto the death."

Peace

Thou will keep him in perfect peace
Whose mind is stayed upon Thee!
Thou will keep him in perfect peace
Whose mind is stayed upon Thee!
So seek peace and pursue it with all thine heart…
So seek peace and pursue it with all thine heart…
And you will come to know
The Peace of God—that keeps you faithfully!
And you will come to know
The Peace of God—that keeps you faithfully!
Don't worry 'bout anything,
But pray about everything!
Tell God all your needs…
Don't worry 'bout anything,
But pray about everything!
Tell God all your needs…
And don't forget to thank Him
When His answers come to you;
And you will find the Peace of God
Will find your heart's needs too!
And the Peace of God in Jesus Christ
Will guard your heart and mind…
And the Peace of God in Jesus Christ
Will guard your heart and mind!
No greater source in all the earth
Of peace you'll ever find!
No greater source in all the earth
Of peace you'll ever find!
So seek peace and pursue it with all thine heart…
So seek peace and pursue it with all thine heart…
Thou will keep him in perfect peace
Whose mind is stayed upon Thee!
Thou will keep him in perfect peace
Whose mind is stayed upon Thee!
Thou will keep him in perfect peace
Whose mind is stayed upon Thee!
(Based on Isaiah 26:3; Psalm 34:14 KJV; Philippians 4:6-7 The Living Bible)

Song of Thanksgiving

Holy…Holy…
Holy…Holy…
Lord, You are worthy…You're worthy of my praise!
Lord, You are worthy…My voice to You I raise!

Worthy…Worthy…
Worthy…Worthy…
Worthy is The Lamb…To receive all my praise!
Worthy is The Lamb…My heart to You I raise!

Seek You…Seek You…
Seek You…Seek You…
Lord, I want to seek You, to know You more and more!
Lord, I want to seek You, I open my heart's door…
Lord, I want to seek You, I open my heart's door!

Seek You…Seek You…
Seek You…Seek You…
Seek You in the morning…I'll seek You at noon…
Seek You in the evening…'til I come to know You!

Jesus…Jesus…
Jesus…Jesus…
Lord, You are here now…I hear You call my name!
Lord, You are here now…And I'll never be the same!
Lord, You are here now…And I'll never be the same!

Thank You…Thank You…
Thank You…Thank You…
Thank You for Your goodness!
I thank You for Your Grace!
Thank You Lord, You touched me;
And I saw You face to face!
Thank You Lord, You touched me;
And I saw You face to face!

I Will

I will wait…I will wait upon You.
I will wait…I will wait upon You.
For the answer's on its way!
As I listen and pray…
I will wait…I will wait upon You!

I will keep…I will keep my mind on Thee!
I will keep…I will keep my mind on Thee!
I won't look to circumstance, or what my eyes can see…
But I'll keep…I will keep my mind on Thee!

For the Lord He loves me so!
And He wants me to know
How very special that I am
To the Lord!

I will listen…I will listen to Your voice.
I will listen…I will listen to Your voice.
I will know I've heard from You: Where to go and what to do…
I will listen …I will listen to Your voice!

I will sit…at Your feet each day and pray.
I will sit…at Your feet each day and pray.
Meditate on Your Word…'til my heart is reassured!
I will sit…at Your feet each day and pray!

For the Lord He loves me so!
And He wants me to know
How very special that I am
To the Lord!

What Dream Is In Your Heart?

Perhaps you've been waiting on God to fulfill the hidden desire in your heart. Let me encourage you to not give up on your dream! As I have learned, sometimes our vision needs to die, but then the Lord resurrects it again as we trust Him, and especially as we trust His timing! Although waiting on God's timing is never easy, in the end the fulfillment of the dream will be even that much sweeter.

The Lord has used the final poem in this collection "Water the Seed With Faith," to greatly encourage me to keep believing that His purposes for my life will be realized and that the dream hidden in my heart came from Him. So I just want to remind you that God is no respecter of persons, and what He will do for one of us, He will also do for another, as long as we are seeking Him and seeking to walk in His will. Let your heart be reminded of God's faithfulness, and be encouraged to continually walk by faith because God is on your side. We are reminded in Psalms 37:23, "The steps of a good man are ordered by the Lord: and he delighteth in his way."

Lord, I pray that "Water the Seed With Faith," will encourage your people as much as it has encouraged me.

Water the Seed With Faith

Hear the word of the Lord,
He's just spoken to your heart…
Believe and you'll receive,
Or doubt and do without!
Not based on selfish desires
Or what are wants, not needs…
But based upon the will of God;
The Word He's given as seeds
Planted in your spirit man
And rooted in your soul;
Springing forth to your understanding,
To bring you to His goal…
Of manifesting in your life today,
All He's planned for you…
And bringing you into His purpose
For which He's created you!
See the fruits that you will bear
As gifts from God above,
Because He's called you to a purpose,
And He's called your name in love.
Because He's called you to obedience,
To diligently seek His face…
And He's a rewarder of seekers
Whom have tasted of His grace!
Not the casual inquirer, but…
One who's given his whole heart…
To know the Lord and His ways,
In fullness, and <u>not</u> in part.
So hear the word of the Lord today,
And the seed will sprout and grow.
Then contemplate in faith again
As the fruit begins to flow!
Remember to give Him the glory
So everyone will surely know…
That the hand of the Lord has done this…
Through His vessel…His Glory to show!
(Psalms 109:27) "That they may know that
this is Thy hand; That Thou Lord hast done it."